Learning About
Castles and Palaces

by Ruth Shannon Odor
illustrated by Lydia Halverson

CHILDRENS PRESS, CHICAGO

Library of Congress Cataloging in Publication Data

Odor, Ruth Shannon.
  Learning about castles and palaces.

  (Learning about series)
  Summary: Text and illustrations describe
several castles and palaces in Europe, from
cold and drafty fortresses to the elegance of
such places as the Schönbrunn Palace in Vienna.
   1. Castles—Europe—Juvenile literature.
2. Palaces—Europe—Juvenile literature.
[1. Castles. 2. Palaces] I. Halverson, Lydia,
ill. II. Title. III. Series.
D910.5.O36 1982   940   82-9567
ISBN 0-516-06537-8

Copyright© 1982 by Regensteiner Publishing Enterprises, Inc.
All rights reserved. Published simultaneously in Canada.
Printed in the United States of America.
1 2 3 4 5 6 7 8 9 10 R 91 90 89 88 87 86 85 84 83 82

Learning About Castles and Palaces

Created by THE CHILD'S WORLD

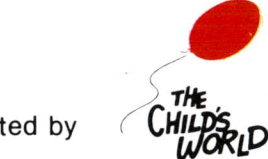

Knights in shining armor. Ladies in flowing gowns. Soaring battlements. Tall stone towers. Fairy tales and magic. Gold, glitter, and romance!

You're daydreaming about castles, of course. And you're wishing you lived in one. There, you'd find adventure—and fun!

Adventure? Yes. Fun? Not always. For a medieval castle was a fortress as well as a home. And the first castles were often drafty, damp places. Prisoners sometimes moaned in dark dungeons. There was fierce fighting when an enemy attacked—and fear and starvation during a siege.

Not every castle was Camelot!

The first castles were built in what is now France and Germany. That was about 1000 years ago. Before then, Rome ruled the known world. But in 476 A.D., Rome's empire fell. In the centuries that followed, Vikings swooped down on Europe. Landowners began building walls to protect their land. (And to stay alive!)

Even after the danger of these raids was over, nobles built castles to control areas of land. They didn't know how to build strong stone forts like the forts the Romans had built. So they built castles of earth and wood. And they built them quickly.

These early castles were called motte-and-bailey castles. "Motte" means "mound." A "bailey" was the yard inside the walls. A stockade, or wooden wall, was built around the castle.

A bridge was built over a ditch. It led to the gate of the bailey. Another bridge was built over a ditch at the rear of the bailey. It led to the mound. It also led to the building on top.

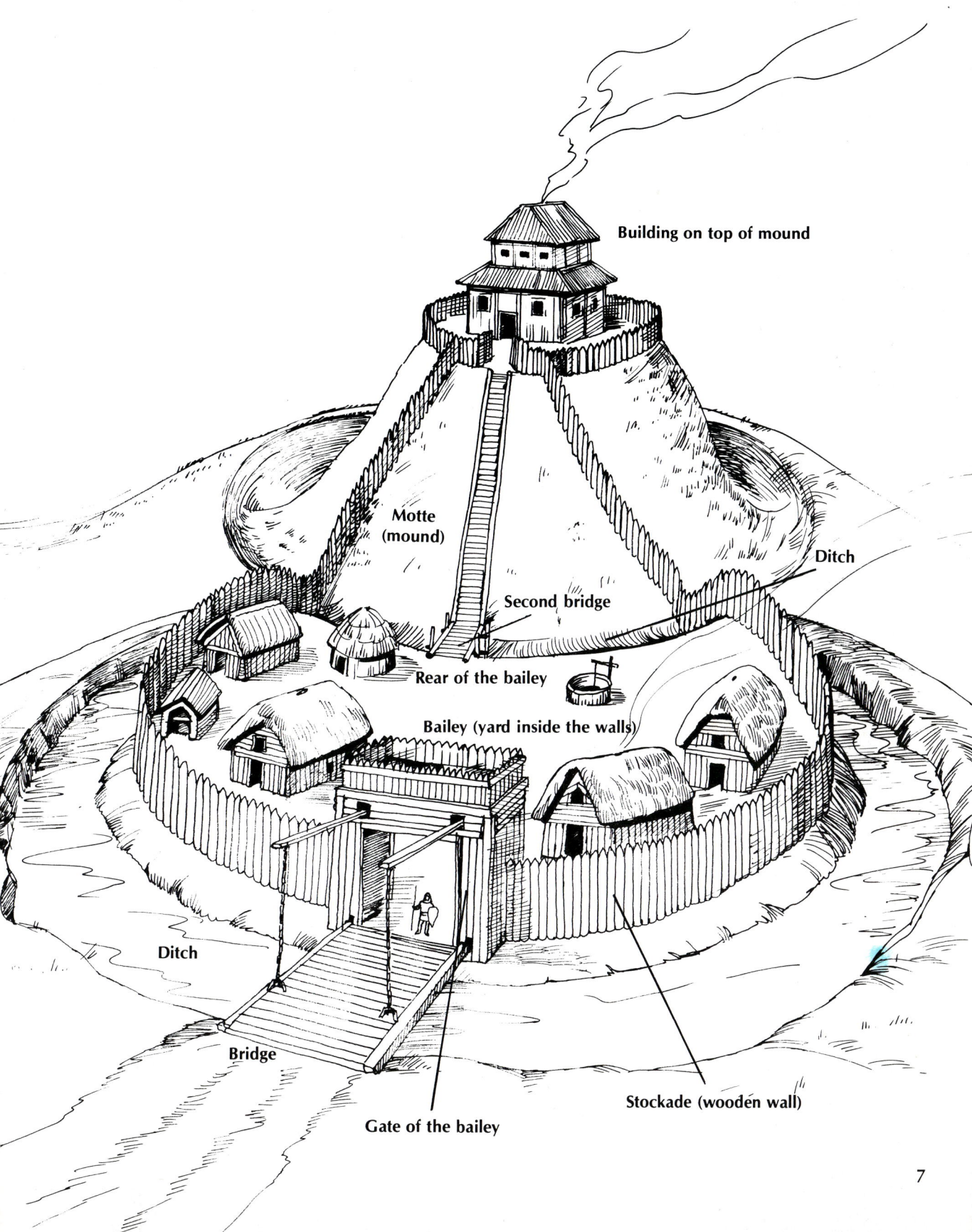

The motte-and-bailey castle came to England in 1066. It came when Norman invaders landed on the coast of England at Pevensey.

Armed men jumped out and waded to shore. Their leader, Duke William of Normandy, had led them across 70 miles of water to invade England. William had decided that he wanted to rule more than Normandy. He wanted to be the next king of England.

Duke William brought a premade castle with him! (Wood pieces had been cut and pegs had been made for putting the pieces together.) In one day William built a castle at Hastings! Before that day, not many castles had been built in England.

William was successful in the invasion. And he soon conquered all of England. (That's why he was called William the Conqueror!)

William had his lords build castles to protect themselves and house their soldiers. By 1100 there were thousands of motte-and-bailey castles in England. In 1137, someone wrote, "They filled the land full of castles."

THE AGE OF CASTLES

Motte-and-baily castles were easily built. They were also easily destroyed! So before long, castle builders began using stone instead of wood.

Castles became fortresses. Most of them were built on high hills overlooking mountain passes. Others were built on steep cliffs. Some were built on islands.

Other times, though, a castle had to be built where there were no natural defenses. Man-made defenses were necessary.

A moat was one way a castle dweller kept enemies out. A moat was a deep ditch that was dug around the castle. It was filled with water . . . and sometimes with crocodiles! A drawbridge was built across the moat. (A drawbridge is a bridge that can be raised and lowered.)

Here's how a castle may have looked in the Middle Ages.

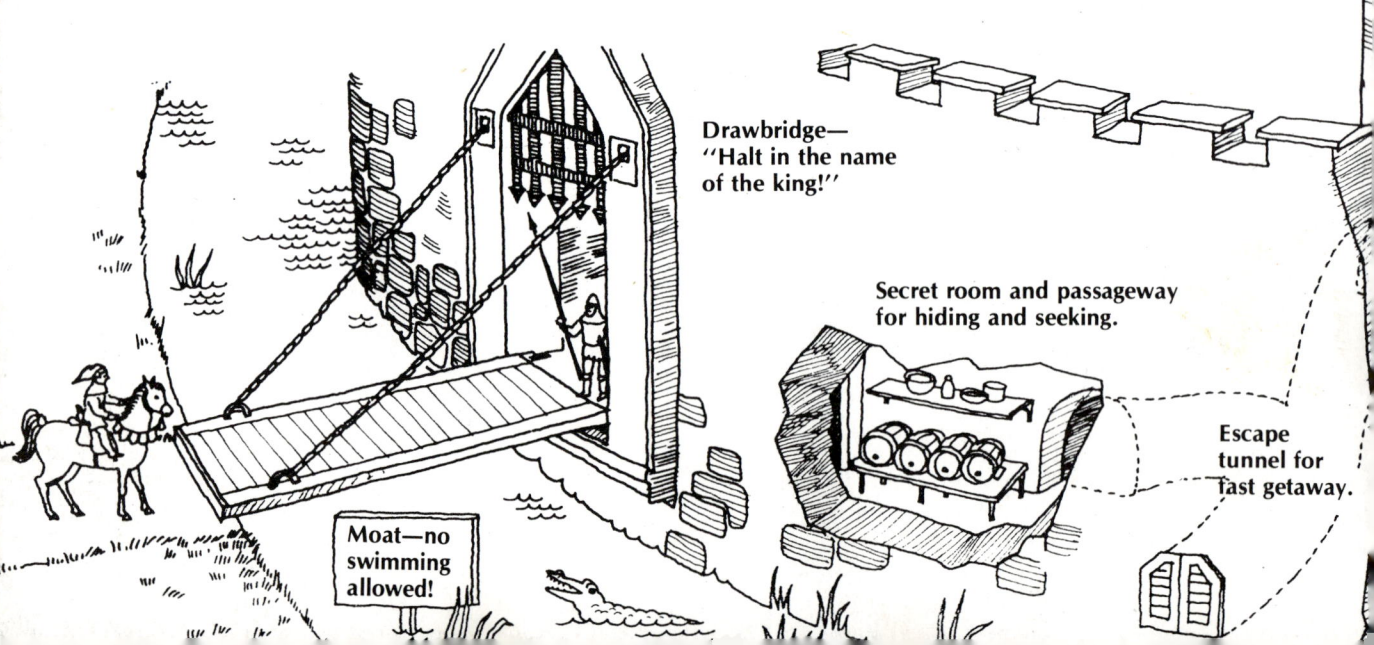

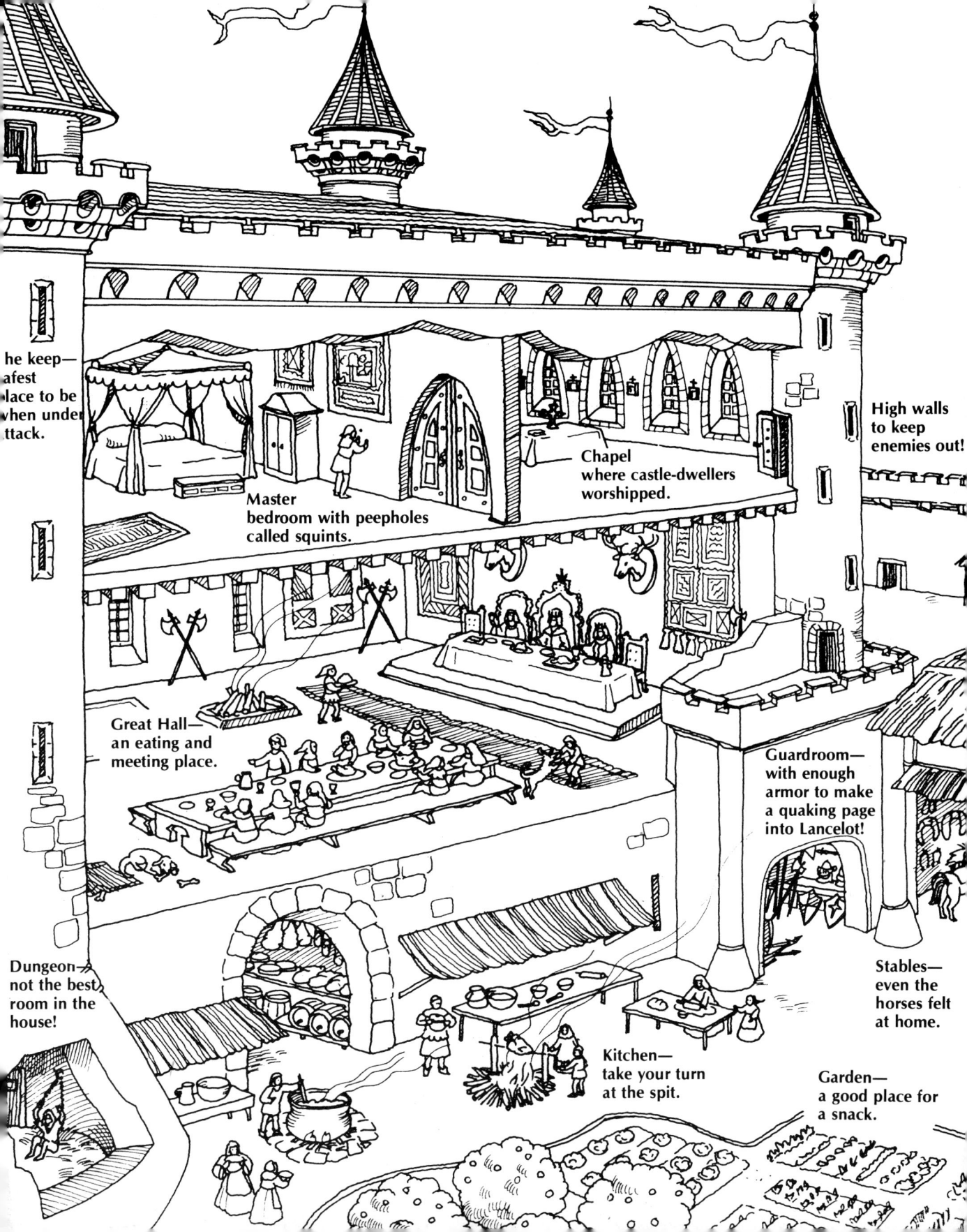

Castles came alive at daybreak. Servants lighted the fires in the great hall and the kitchen. Men-at-arms climbed up to the battlements to relieve those who had kept the night watch. The lord and lady dressed and attended mass in the chapel.

Then came breakfast. It was a small meal—only bread and wine or ale. After breakfast everyone went to work!

The lord had meetings with his head servant and other workers. After that, he might go hunting.

Hunting was a favorite sport in the Middle Ages. And falconry was a favorite way to hunt. The falcon, or hawk, could bring down birds that flew beyond the range of an arrow. Every lord had his falcons. Often a lord carried his favorite falcon to chapel. It would ride on his wrist.

The lady spent her day overseeing the servants. She would also sew and talk with guests. Sometimes she joined the hunt.

Children did schoolwork. They were tutored by the chaplain or by one of his clerks. After lessons were done, the girls played with dolls. The boys played with balls, tops, or bows and arrows.

Knights and squires practiced fencing. (Fencing is the art of sword-fighting.)

Grooms fed the horses and swept the stables. The smith made horseshoes and nails. Servants cleaned and cared for the many rooms in the castle. The laundress did the washing. The cook and his staff turned the meat on a spit. They made stews and baked huge pies.

SOME FAMOUS CASTLES

Not many people live in castles anymore. But some castles have stayed in the family! The oldest inhabited castle in the world is

WINDSOR CASTLE

Britain's royal family's name comes from this castle. And Queen Elizabeth lives there at least part of the time. (Windsor is 23 miles west of London.) For 900 years Windsor has been one of the principal homes of the king or queen.

Windsor was built by William the Conqueror. Its first form was motte-and-bailey. Later, King Henry II built a round stone tower on the mound. Down through the years, kings added to, rebuilt, and restored the castle. The result is a huge grouping of different structures.

A legend has grown up around Windsor. The ghost of Herne the Hunter is said to haunt Windsor some nights. Herne was Richard I's forester. The ghost rides a black horse. And . . . some say . . . he's been spotted in the forest around Windsor.

Prince Charles was made Prince of Wales at
CAERNARVON CASTLE
in July, 1969, by his mother, Queen Elizabeth II.

The history of Caernarvon Castle began during the reign of King Edward I of England. In order to conquer Wales, he established a number of new towns. Each town was occupied by English settlers and guarded by a castle. These castles became known as Edwardian castles. They were strong military structures.

The most famous of these castles is Caernarvon. Today the walls and towers are almost as they were when they were built long ago. But inside, only the foundations of the building are left.

Castles seem to promote storytelling. Sir Walter Scott wrote a famous story about

KENILWORTH CASTLE

in England. Scott's novel, *Kenilworth,* is a romance. It involves cover-up, confusion, and murder. The story is set during the reign of Queen Elizabeth I.

The castle itself began as a tower but ended up larger and more elaborate. The water area alone around the castle covered 111 acres.

Once the castle held out for seven months against the whole army of England. That was in 1266. The lord of the castle, Simon de Montfort, finally surrendered. His men were starving.

Not a "storybook" but a real live prince and princess sometimes can be seen at

BALMORAL CASTLE

This Scottish castle is one of the private homes of Britain's king or queen and family. Prince Charles and his wife, Diana, sometimes stay at Balmoral.

Queen Victoria's family was the first royal family to live in the castle. Prince Albert bought the property and had the castle built for Victoria. Each year the family came to Balmoral to hunt grouse.

Although Balmoral is called a castle, it is more like a palace, for it is more a home than a fort.

Another royal home is famous for a different reason. It is said that the stones of

GLAMIS CASTLE

in Scotland look blood red in the northern sunset. Perhaps people say that because of Glamis' blood-red history.

At Glamis, King Duncan was murdered. William Shakespeare tells the tale in his play, "Macbeth."

And at the same castle, a Lady Glamis was accused of witchcraft. She also was accused of plotting to poison King James V. Lady Glamis was burned at the stake. (Legend says that her son later proved her innocence.)

Not all of Glamis' history is dark. The castle was the childhood home of Lady Elizabeth Bowes-Lyon. She married King George VI of England and became the mother of the present Queen Elizabeth. Glamis Castle is the birthplace of Queen Elizabeth's sister, Margaret.

Also in Scotland is the famous

EDINBURGH CASTLE

This castle stands on a rock. The incline is so steep that it has been climbed only three times. (Would you like to give it a try?) Once was in 1313 when the Earl of Moray and 30 of his followers climbed the rock. They surprised the English soldiers and took the castle. Then their Scottish King, Robert the Bruce, ruled.

The 1000-year-old castle became the chief fortress of the kings of Scotland. Around it grew the town that became the capital city.

And in Ireland you can kiss the Blarney Stone at

BLARNEY CASTLE

Blarney Castle overlooks the River Martin. This castle is known all over the world. Its fame is due to a certain stone in its battlements.

A legend is told about the stone. When someone kisses it, he receives powers of great speech. (The word "blarney" means flattery.)

But don't go to Blarney unless you are daring. It takes nerve to kiss the stone. You have to hang upside down from the battlements!

A play, not a stone, is one reason why Denmark's

KRONBORG CASTLE

is famous. Shakespeare chose Kronborg Castle as the setting for his play, "Hamlet."

In the play, Hamlet, Prince of Denmark, lived in the castle. One night a ghost appeared and talked to Hamlet. It was the ghost of his father.

Hamlet's father told him that he had not died naturally as was thought. He had been murdered. And the murderer was Hamlet's uncle. Hamlet promised that he would revenge his father's death.

A lot of real-life drama occurred at

COUCY CASTLE

in northern France. Robber barons lived in it during the 12th century. These barons used their power and their castle to rob those who passed through their land. Travelers in the days of knights and castles could have told many tales of castle-owning bandits!

Besides its wicked tenants, Coucy Castle was noted for the roofs on its four towers. Each tower roof looked like a witch's hat. The castle was damaged during World War I. But tales about it are still told.

Tales are also told about how the Old Belgian castle called

THE CASTLE OF THE COUNTS

grew and grew and grew. In 870 Count (or Prince) Baldwin built a castle on a small island. The city of Ghent grew up around the castle.

In 1180 Count Philip made the castle larger. It then had over 20 towers. Years later the Castle of the Counts changed again. It was made into a house for the knights of the Order of the Golden Fleece.

Today the castle holds many kinds of tools once used to torture enemies and prisoners held in dungeons.

A king who wished he *had* lived in the medieval days of castles and knights built his own castles. One of those castles is

NEUSCHWANSTEIN

This castle rests between huge mountains in Bavaria, Germany. Its name means "The New Castle of the Swan."

King Ludwig II chose that name because of one of his favorite stories. It was the story of Lohengrin. Lohengrin was a brave knight who traveled in a boat pulled by a swan. Lohengrin rescued a princess. Ludwig liked to pretend he was Lohengrin.

Besides Neuschwanstein, Ludwig built two other castles. All three were beautiful . . . and costly. The throne rooms in the castles were decorated with scenes from the story of Lohengrin.

The Bavarian people loved their tall, handsome king. At first they didn't seem to mind that he lived in his dreams and his strange castles. But as time passed, many felt that the king had spent too much money. In 1886, a committee declared Ludwig insane. He died the same year.

Walt Disney patterned his fairy-tale castles after Neuschwanstein. You'll find the Sleeping Beauty Castle at Disneyland in California, and the Cinderella Castle at Disney World in Florida.

A castle so strong it was never taken by direct attack was the

CASTLE OF THE KNIGHTS

(Krak des Chevaliers)

in Syria. This castle, which was very famous, was built in 1131 by a group of Crusaders. They were knights who had the job of protecting pilgrims traveling to the Holy Land.

The castle was built to withstand attack from all directions. It had hidden openings for attacking enemies. There were also underground passages, and huge storage cellars. The cellars could hold enough food for 2000 men for a whole year.

But while the castle was strong and was never taken by direct attack, it did fall. Why?

The sultan attacking the castle used trickery. He had a letter forged. The letter ordered the castle to surrender. It was "signed" (forged, of course) by the head of the crusader knights. It was delivered by carrier pigeon.

The commander of the castle must have known that the letter was a trick. But he also knew that the Crusaders were being driven out of Palestine. This meant he could get no help from outside. While the attackers couldn't break through the castle walls, those inside were trapped. Sooner or later they would run out of food. So the commander ordered his men to surrender.

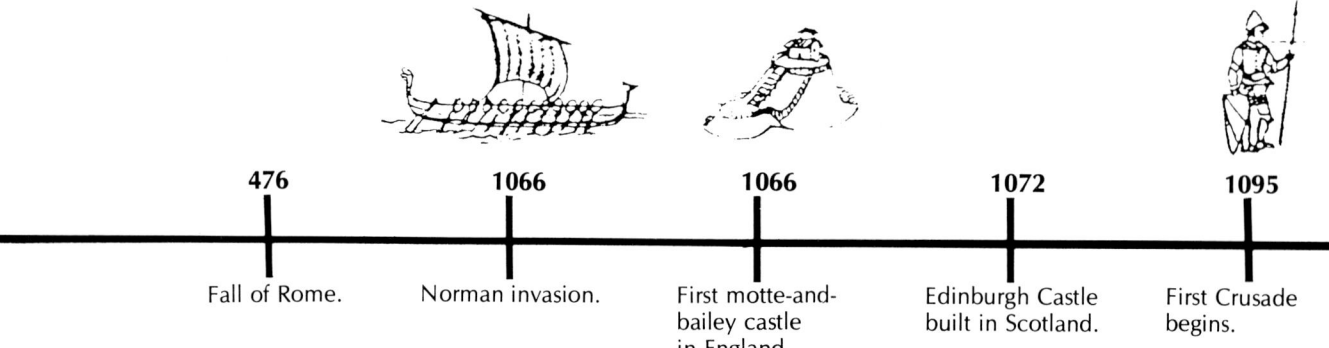

476	1066	1066	1072	1095
Fall of Rome.	Norman invasion.	First motte-and-bailey castle in England.	Edinburgh Castle built in Scotland.	First Crusade begins.

THE END OF THE AGE OF CASTLES

There came a time when the age of castles was over. Why?

• Gunpowder was invented. Methods of fighting wars changed. Instead of bows and arrows, there were guns. Instead of battering rams, there were cannons. Guns blew soldiers and knights right off battlements! Cannons made holes in walls and towers!

• The system of government changed. Strong nations did not need castles to protect land from invaders.

Some castles were torn down by kings. Others were just left to fall into ruins. But many were turned into great houses or palaces.

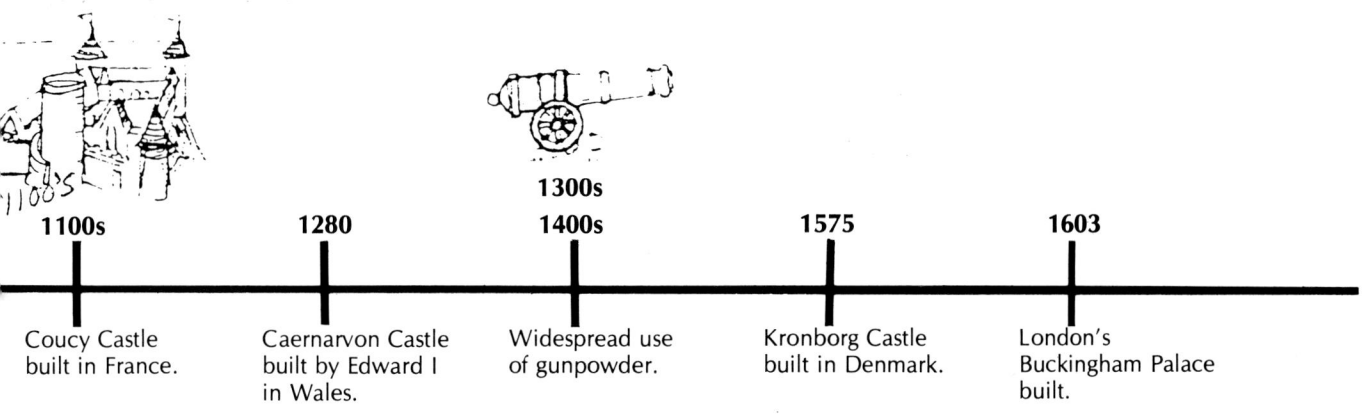

1100s	1280	1300s 1400s	1575	1603
Coucy Castle built in France.	Caernarvon Castle built by Edward I in Wales.	Widespread use of gunpowder.	Kronborg Castle built in Denmark.	London's Buckingham Palace built.

THE BEGINNING OF PALACES

A palace is the home of royalty. A king or queen, an emperor or empress, a sultan, a shah, a shogun, a pharaoh may live in a palace. Or a palace may be a building where a ruler conducts his duties. And sometimes a palace is just a stately house.

Palaces come in all different shapes and designs, depending upon the country and period of time in which they were built. Some are low and flat-roofed. Some are tall and peaked. Others are domed, round, or rectangular.

Palaces are very much like castles—except they do not need huge walls to keep invaders out.

SOME FAMOUS PALACES

Britain's royal family lives in

BUCKINGHAM PALACE

Tourists flock to London's Buckingham Palace at 10:30 a.m. each day. They go to see the Changing of the Guard. This takes place every morning when the royal family is home. A new group of guards in uniforms march out. They take over the duties of those who have been on guard through the night.

The land on which the palace stands was once covered with 30,000 mulberry trees. (King James I was trying to produce silk in England. It didn't work.) The area became a loitering place. It was known as Mulberry Garden.

In 1703 the Duke of Buckingham built a mansion there. King George III bought the building for a palace. George IV had many improvements made on the building. The next ruler was Queen Victoria. She had the palace made even larger.

The palace contains a throne room, ballroom, and royal apartments. There is also a chapel, and a picture gallery. (Not a bad place to live!) But you aren't allowed inside to visit. After all it is the *home* of Queen Elizabeth and her family.

Mary, Queen of Scots, lived in

HOLYROOD PALACE

Holyrood, in Edinburgh, Scotland, looks more like a castle than a palace. The teen-aged Mary returned to this palace after the death of her first husband. Her first husband was the king of France, Frances II. Mary had been sent from Scotland to be educated in France. There she met and married Frances II.

Mary spent only six years at Holyrood. Those years were filled with violence. Mary's second husband had her secretary and friend killed. Later he was murdered.

Finally, Mary was forced to leave her throne as Queen of Scotland. She fled to England. There, she too met a tragic death. (She was beheaded on orders from Queen Elizabeth I.)

This beautiful waterside scene shows the

STOCKHOLM ROYAL PALACE

at night!

The site on which this palace stands is the place where Stockholm began. But the Royal Palace isn't the original palace. It was preceded by Three Crowns Palace. All but one wing of Three Crowns burned down in 1697.

Today you can visit the Royal Palace. It's open to tourists year-around! And if you visit the museum, you'll see bits of the original palace. Artifacts have been carefully preserved. Also inside the museum are many other historic and artistic treasures.

The world's most famous palace is

VERSAILLES

in France. It was built by Louis XIV. He was the ruler of France when it was the most powerful country in Europe. He called himself the Sun King.

Louis did not like living in Paris, the capital city. He preferred his father's hunting lodge in the country, outside Paris. So Louis decided to turn the lodge into a palace. He wanted to make it so grand that it would astonish the world. And he did!

The Palace of Versailles can house 5000 people. The walls and ceilings are made of marble. The doors are carved and gilded. The staircases are huge. Rare paintings and statues make it grand, as do the formal gardens with their flowers, shrubs and fountains. Even today the formal gardens are planted with blooming flowers that form the letter "L" for Louis.

A famous part of the palace is the Hall of Mirrors. It is a great hall decorated with huge mirrors. Such large mirrors were seldom seen in the time of Louis XIV. They were considered priceless. In 1919 the treaty that ended World War I was signed in the Hall of Mirrors.

Today the Palace of Versailles is a museum to the glories of France.

Hall of Mirrors

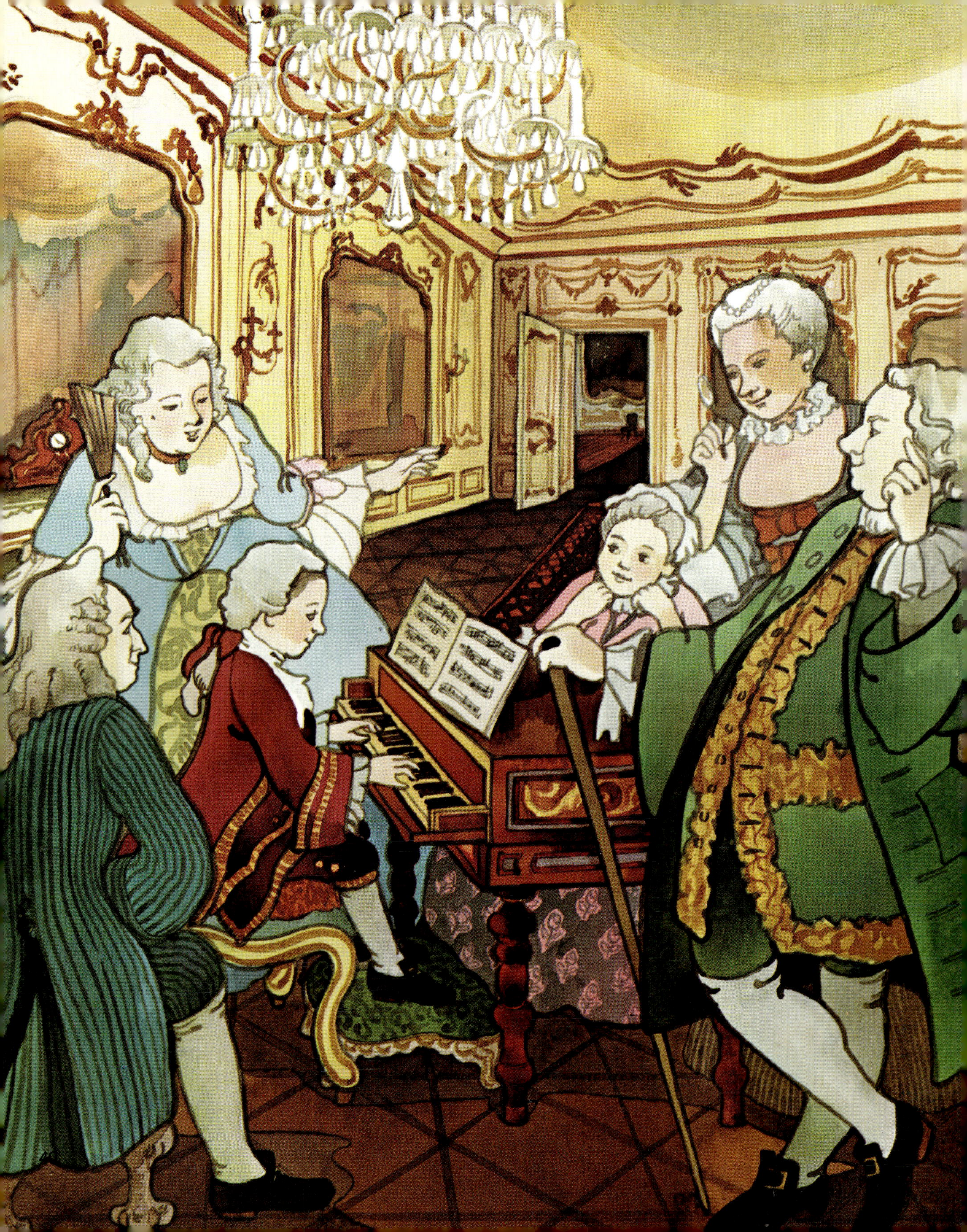

But you haven't seen a palace until you've seen

SCHÖNBRUNN PALACE

in Vienna, Austria. It's E-L-E-G-A-N-T! It was here that the Hapsburgs lived. They were the ruling family of Austria.

This dignified and spacious palace has 1,441 rooms! One of them is a gold and white Grand Gallery. It is full of mirrors and 1,000 candleholders! Many of the rooms contain porcelain stoves that are trimmed with gold.

Empress Maria Theresa loved the Palace of Schönbrunn. It was her favorite home. She and her royal family spent summers at the palace. Here she loved playing with her thirteen children. One of these children was the famous Marie Antoinette.

One special visitor to Schönbrunn was a six-year-old boy. Everyone was amazed at how the boy played the piano. His name was Wolfgang Amadeus Mozart.

Legend says that young Mozart was in love with Marie Antoinette. He supposedly told others he would someday marry her. Had he done so, Marie's life would have been much different—and perhaps longer, too! (She was beheaded, along with her husband, King Louis XVI, during the French Revolution.)

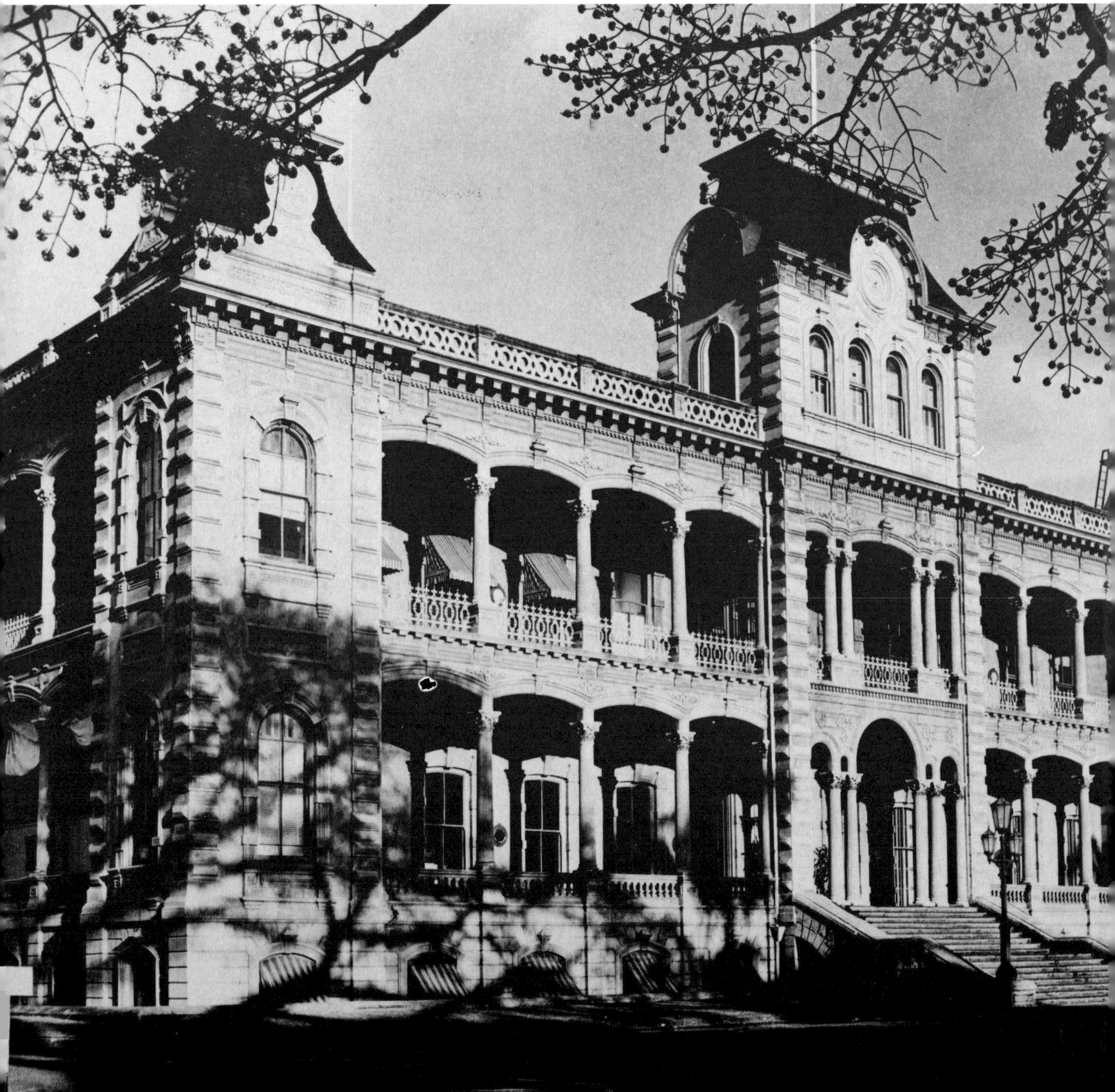

The United States' only claim to a palace is

IOLANI PALACE

in Honolulu, Hawaii. And Iolani is not really a palace. It's a government building. But it was a palace long ago.

The Hawaiian Islands were settled about 2000 years ago by Polynesians who crossed the ocean in canoes. The world knew nothing of them until Captain James Cook located the Islands in 1778.

King Kamehameha I united the islands. He became the first king. The last ruler was a queen. Her name was Liliuokalani. In 1894, Hawaii became a republic. Then it became a United States territory. In 1959, Hawaii became the United State's 50th state.

Old palaces, like old castles, have stories to tell. One story about Iolani is a mystery. Kings of Iolani always went in and out through the King Street Gate. It seems that gate was often found open even when it had been securely locked.

Gatekeepers said that they sometimes had seen ghosts marching through the King Street Gate. They said the ghosts were King Kamehameha III and his men.

The beautiful Palace of Catherine the Great is at

TSARSKOYEO SELO

(Tsars' Village)

in Russia.

Catherine the Great of Russia lived in style in this lovely palace. Trains on the first railroad in Russia stopped in Tsars Village. The trains brought hundreds of pleasure-seekers to the town each summer. They came to attend the dances presided over by Johann Strauss, the great composer of waltzes.

The magnificent summer palace, with its blue and white and gold decorations, tells of the elegance of royalty in days of long ago. Electric lights installed in the palace and the town were the first in commercial service in the world.

The inside of the palace was ruined during war. It, however, has been redone by modern craftsmen. One room, though, could not be replaced. It was called the Amber Room. The paneling was made of carvings in amber with miniatures that were so small they could be seen only with a magnifying glass.

45

Castles and palaces made history. They affected the lives of many people. Today, whether ruins, residences, or tourist attractions, they are romantic reminders of days long ago.

We read about them. We daydream about them. And, sometimes, we wish. . . . Perhaps it would have been fun after all!

INDEX

Antoinette, Marie, 41
Austria, palaces of, 40-41
Balmoral Castle, 19
Belgium, castles of, 26-27
Blarney Castle, 23
Buckingham Palace, 33-34
Caernarvon Castle, 16-17, 32
Camelot, 5
Catherine the Great, 44
Charles, Prince of Wales, 16, 19
Cinderella Castle, 28
Coucy Castle, 25, 33
Counts, The Castle of, 26
Crusaders, 31-32
Denmark, castles of, 24
Diana, Princess of Wales, 19
Disney, Walt, 28
Drawbridge, 10
Dungeons, 5, 10
Edinburgh Castle, 22, 32
Edwardian Castles, 17, 33
Elizabeth I, Queen, 18, 36
Elizabeth II, Queen, 14, 16, 21, 35
England, castles of, 14-18
England, palaces of, 34, 35
France, castles of, 25
France, palaces of, 38-39
Germany, castles of, 28-29
Glamis, 20-21
"Hamlet," 24
Hawaii, palaces of, 42-43
Holyrood Palace, 36
Iolani Palace, 43
Ireland, castles of, 23
Kamehameha I, King, 43
Keep, 10-11
Kenilworth Castle, 18

Knights, 13, 26, 28, 32
Krak des Chevaliers, 31
Kronborg Castle, 24, 32
Lancelot, 11
Liliuokalani, 43
Lohengrin, 28
Louis XIV, King, 38
Ludwig II, King, 28
"Macbeth," 20
Mary, Queen of Scots, 36
Middle Ages, 11, 12
Moat, 10
Motte-and-bailey castle, 6, 8-10, 32
Mozart, Wolfgang, 41
Neuschwanstein Castle, 28
Royal Palace, Stockholm, 37
Russia, palaces of, 44-45
Schönbrunn Palace, 41
Scotland, castles of, 19-22
Scotland, palaces of, 36
Scott, Sir Walter, 18
Shakespeare, William, 20, 24
Sleeping Beauty Castle, 28
Strauss, Johann, 44
Sweden, palaces of, 37
Syria, castles of, 30-31
Tsarskoyeo Selo, 44
Versailles, Palace of, 38
Victoria, Queen, 19, 35
William the Conqueror, 9, 14
Windsor Castle, 14

PHOTO CREDITS

Photos on pages 15, 16, 19, 22, 34 courtesy of the British Tourist Authority
Photo on page 23 courtesy of the Irish Tourist Board
Photo on page 24 courtesy of the Danish Tourist Board
Photo on page 26 courtesy of the Belgian National Tourist Board
Photo on page 29 courtesy of the German National Tourist Office
Photo on page 34 courtesy of Gladys Peterson
Photo on page 37 courtesy of the Swedish National Tourist Office
Photo on page 37 courtesy of Gladys Peterson
Photos on pages 38 and 39 courtesy of the French Cultural Services
Photos on page 42 courtesy of the Hawaii Visitors Bureau
Cover photo courtesy of the German National Tourist Office

DATE DUE			
10/6 110 Paint			
11/12 107 109			
10/31 104			
3/18/09			

95

940 ODO

Odor, Ruth Shannon.

Learning about castles and palaces.

354194 03798D